THE NATURE COMPANY

CREEPY CRAWLIES

In 3-D!

Photographs by David G. Burder
Text by Rick and Susan Sammon

Starrhill Press
Washington, D.C.

A Closer Look

Have you ever really looked at a bug, so you could examine all its different parts and colors? Maybe you thought it was ugly, or maybe you thought it was beautiful. No matter, because the closer you look the more fascinating a bug will become.

The pictures in this book were taken by David Burder with special three-dimensional (3-D) photography. Wear the enclosed 3-D glasses and you will see the pictures come alive. Let the photographs take you on a close-up tour of creepy crawlies like you've never seen them before!

Creepy crawlies are everywhere. There are many more types of insects than any other animal. In fact, there are millions of species! Insects are found in almost every place on earth. They play an important role in the ecological balance of our planet. Without insects, many animals would have no food. And without spiders and their webs, there would be way too many flying insects.

Many creepy crawly habitats, like the rainforest and wetlands, are currently being destroyed. Without a safe home, species will become extinct. Many have already been lost. By protecting their homes, we can protect the creepy crawlies for today's and tomorrow's nature lovers.

If you catch one of these small creatures to observe, please handle it with care and try to release it unharmed.

Rick and Susan Sammon

Croton-on-Hudson, New York

ANTS live with hundreds, even thousands, of other ants in colonies. Ants work together to build their nests, fight off predators, and find food. They communicate by touch and smell. Even though scientists have been studying ants for many years, they are still amazed at how well ants cooperate.

HABITAT

Most ants live in complex tunnels in the ground and in wood. Carpenter ants can ruin trees and decks around houses. Some ants are able to survive underwater for days.

FOOD

Many types of ants like to drink a sweet liquid called honeydew. Honeydew is made by tiny insects called aphids. Some ants "farm" aphids. Ants help protect the aphids and their eggs so the ant colony will have a supply of honeydew.

PHYSICAL CHARACTERISTICS

Ants are strong and tough. Working as a team, they can kill insects many times their size.

FUN FACT

A queen ant lays about a million eggs during its life. Some queens live for 15 years.

MILLIPEDE

MILLIPEDE means a thousand legs, but, in fact, the millipede bug never has more than 400 legs. Still, that's quite a lot! Millipedes are very fast runners and are hard to catch. These creepy crawlies are closely related to the centipede, which has only 30 legs. Millipedes are harmless to humans, while centipedes can inflict a painful bite.

HABITAT

Millipedes are about four inches long. They have hard and flat bodies. They wiggle under rocks, stones, and logs, where they usually make their home.

FOOD

Most millipedes love to eat vegetables and fruit. In a garden they slide into cabbage and lettuce and tunnel into carrots, tomatoes, and strawberries. When you see a small hole in one of these fruits or vegetables, a millipede may be inside.

FUN FACTS

Young millipedes have only six legs. To scare predators some millipedes give off a bad smell when disturbed. Millipedes curl up into a tight ball when frightened. This makes it hard for attackers to eat them.

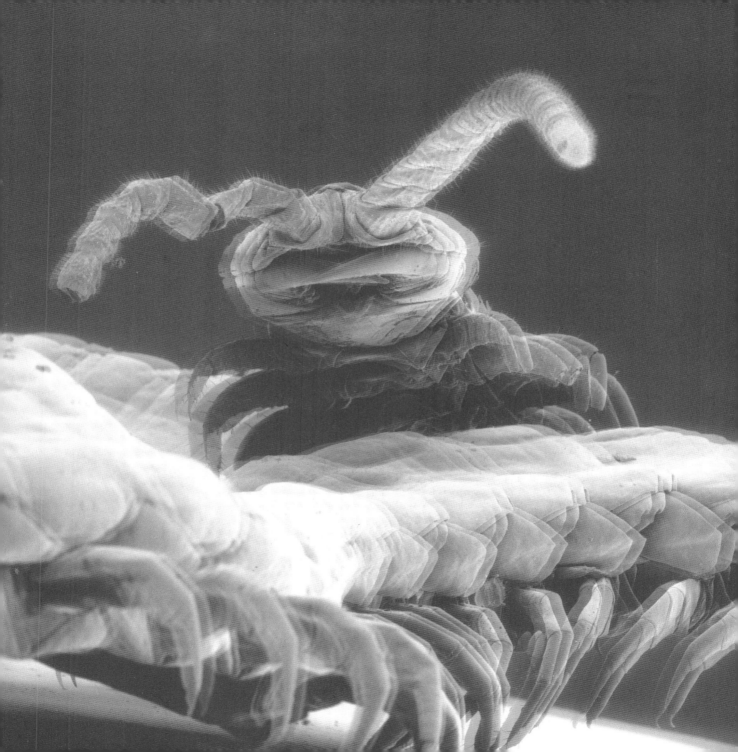

MOSQUITOES have hundreds of hairs on their antennae. The hairs help them sense even the slightest movement. That's how mosquitoes avoid being swatted. The *zizzing* noise a mosquito makes is the sound of the insect's wings beating.

HABITAT
Mosquitoes live in still water—ponds, marshes, puddles, and water-filled flowers. Most mosquitoes live only a few days because they are eaten by birds, bats, dragonflies, and other insects. The ones that avoid predators might live through a winter.

FOOD
Mosquitoes love to drink the juice of oranges, apples, plums, and other fruits. They also like nectar from flowers.

BEHAVIOR
Before they lay eggs, female mosquitoes drink human or other animal blood. The female pierces skin with a sharp, sliding needle inside a long sucking tube. Then the mosquito mixes its saliva with the victim's blood, which makes the blood thinner and easier to suck up. A mosquito bite itches because the saliva contains a mild venom. The saliva can also contain germs of dangerous diseases which the mosquito picked up from its last victim.

SPRINGTAILS

SPRINGTAILS cannot fly. They have no wings, and they can only crawl very, very slowly. So how do they escape predators? They spring from place to place on a tube-like foot. Fossils tell us that these microscopic insects are very primitive. Their distant relatives, the world's first insects, appeared about 300 million years ago.

HABITAT

There are more than 2,000 species of springtails. They live all over the world—even in Antarctica. When they gather on the surface of the snow, they are called snow fleas. On water they are called pond fleas. Springtails live in all sorts of damp places, like beneath rocks and on the underside of dead animals.

FOOD

Springtails love vegetable gardens. They attack seeds, mushrooms, cucumbers, and spinach. Some springtails eat bacteria.

FUN FACT

If you live around a body of water, there are probably lots and lots of springtails around, but they are too small to be seen without a microscope.

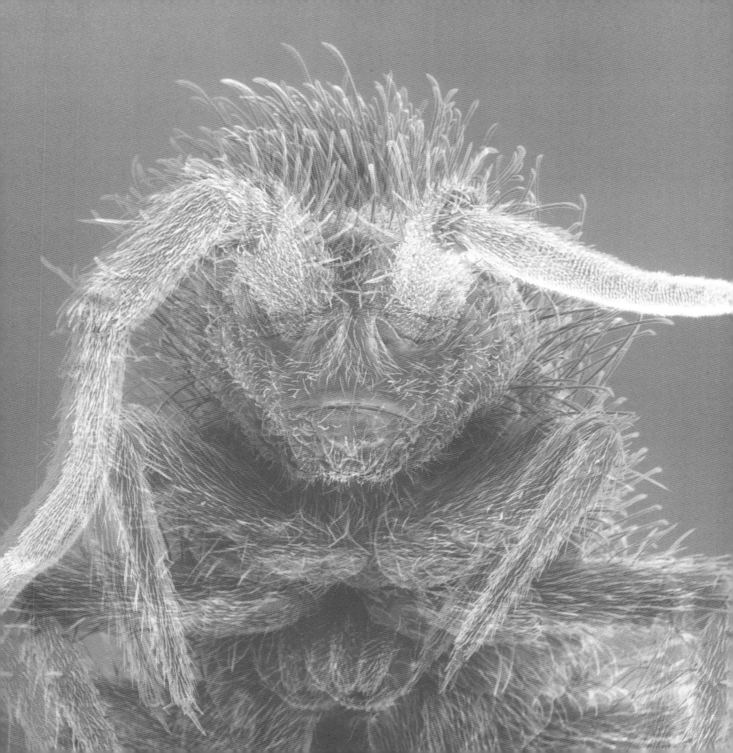

MITES

MITES are miniature relatives of spiders, scorpions, and ticks. Like ticks, mites bite their animal victims and suck out blood or fluid. While sucking the mite can grow to four times its original size. Mites are sensitive to even the slightest amount of heat. They know when a person or animal is walking in the woods or in tall grass. When they sense body heat, mites hitch a ride on their victim.

 HABITAT
Mites live almost anywhere—in the nostrils of seals, in the gills of fish, and even in a moth's "ears." Some mites also live on plants, algae, fungus, and moss.

 BEHAVIOR
A mite called a chigger can eat into your skin and inject a venom that causes a bad itch. If you scratch the itch, the skin around the bite will get hard and protect the mite. When the mite is finished eating, it will fall off by itself. The itch mite is even more annoying than the chigger. It lays eggs under the skin which hatch in two or three days.

 FUN FACT
One type of mite only eats rotten cheese.

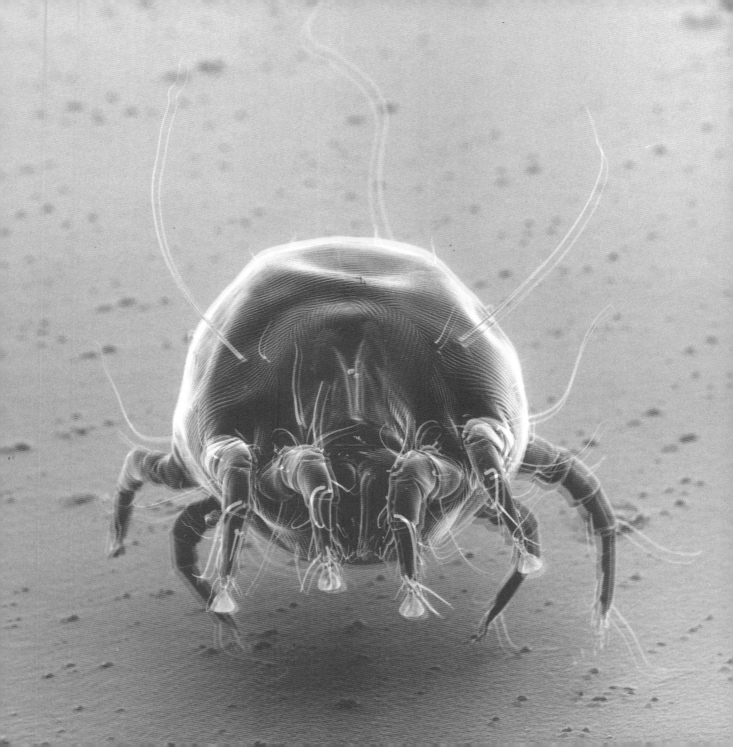

BUTTERFLIES begin life as eggs. Then they hatch into caterpillars. After the caterpillars have eaten enough to become very fat, they make strong cocoons or form chrysalises. Finally, they come out of their cocoons or chrysalises as beautiful insects, with delicate wings.

FOOD

Adult butterflies feed on plant liquids, like nectar, which they suck up through a feeding tube. As caterpillars, they eat the leaves and buds of many plants.

PHYSICAL CHARACTERISTICS

Many butterflies are brightly colored. Some are deep red and almost invisible in the dark, tropical rain forest. Some have transparent wings that make them hard to see. Others look completely different when seen from the top or bottom. If a bird is chasing this type of butterfly, all the butterfly has to do is land on a branch and fold up its wings to disappear from the bird's sight!

SCIENCE EXTRA

Many species of butterflies live in the world's rainforests. More and more rainforest is destroyed every day for timber and farmland. When their rainforest habitat is gone, many species of butterflies will become extinct.

FLEAS

FLEAS are bloodsuckers. They prey on wild animals, birds, and pets. Sometimes they will bite people. A close-up view of a flea shows us the features of what scientists call a true insect. Like other insects, fleas have six-jointed legs and a protective, hard, outer skin called an exoskeleton. They also have wings, as do many insects.

HABITAT
Fleas are found on dogs, cats, and wild animals. Fleas also live on warm tropical beaches. Fleas are sometimes called "no see 'ems" because you can feel the fleas bite, but they are too small to see.

BEHAVIOR
Some fleas can jump several feet—from a dog to your living room couch—in a split second.

SCIENCE EXTRA
These days most fleas don't carry dangerous diseases. But in the Middle Ages fleas carried plagues from Asia to Europe. The diseases killed thousands of people in less than 30 years.

CRICKETS

CRICKETS chirp by rubbing their wings and legs together. By shifting its wings, a cricket can make the chirping sound like it's coming from a different direction. This makes it hard to find a cricket, even if it's in your own room.

HABITAT
There are about 2,000 species of crickets. They live in fields, caves, marshes, and sometimes in your house!

PHYSICAL CHARACTERISTICS
Baby crickets are born in early summer. Like their parents they have an exoskeleton, but they are much smaller and have no wings. Over the summer the young cricket grows fast and sheds its exoskeleton five times. A cricket's powerful legs help it jump to safety when attacked. Some crickets can jump 20 inches—10 times their body length.

FUN FACTS
Crickets' ears are in their legs. The chirp of some crickets can be heard for more than one mile. Only male crickets make the chirping sound.

BEES sting, and the stings punch a one-two wallop. First the sharp point pricks the skin. Then the stinger injects a painful venom into the wound. A bee's stinger is almost too small to see. In this picture, the stinger is enlarged thousands of times. Even with this super close-up photograph, it's hard to see the 10 barbs on the stinger that make it tough to remove from skin.

BEHAVIOR

Bees are not naturally aggressive. They sting people to protect their beehives. They also sting when they are frightened or hurt, like when they are accidentally stepped upon.

PHYSICAL CHARACTERISTICS

Only female bees can sting. Male bees, called drones, don't even have stingers. You can tell males from females because the males have a coat of soft, brown down. If a bee's stinger is torn from its body while stinging, the bee dies.

SCIENCE EXTRA

Some people are allergic to bee stings. If stung, they should take antihistamine medicine to prevent them from getting very, very sick.

SPIDERS are born knowing how to survive. Adult spiders don't have to show young spiders how to walk, make a web, eat, or hide from predators.

HABITAT
Many spiders like to make their webs around lights where there are lots of moths to catch. Spiders also spin webs in trees and in tall grass. One type of spider uses its silk to make a hidden door over its home in the ground. When the spider hears an insect, it peeks out to see what's happening. If the spider is hungry, it will pounce on the insect and drag it down into its home.

PREY
Most spiders spin silky webs that trap moths and other insects. Once an insect is stuck in the web, the spider shakes the web very hard. (Some spiders can tell which type of insect they've caught by how the web wiggles.) The harder the insect struggles, the more tangled up it becomes. Once the insect is exhausted, the spider sucks out its insides, or, wraps it up to save for later.

FUN FACT
Some spiders make silk "balloons" that help them float through the air to find new homes and food.

FLIES have only two wings. Insects like the dragonfly and butterfly are not considered true flies because they have four wings. On their two strong wings, flies can travel longer and faster than any other insect.

HABITAT
Flies are found at the North and South Poles and everywhere in between. They live in garbage cans and on rotting plants and animals.

PHYSICAL CHARACTERISTICS
Flies' huge eyes help them see while flying fast. These huge eyes have hundreds of facets that can detect even the slightest movement from a great distance. Flies have sticky pads on their legs that help them walk upside down on the ceiling.

SCIENCE EXTRA
There are many different types of flies. In some parts of the world, flies spread dangerous diseases, like sleeping sickness and yellow fever. Almost all flies carry germs and should be chased away from picnic food.

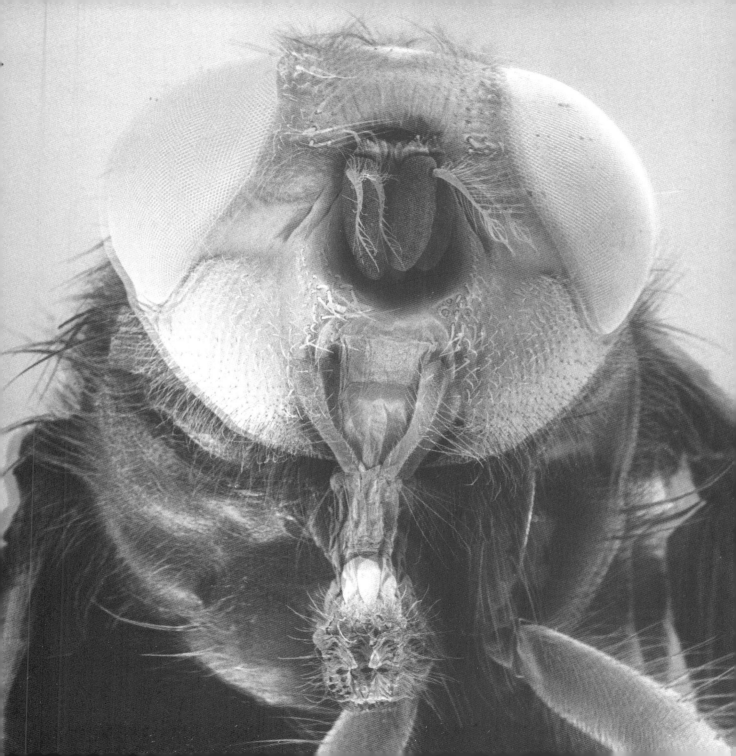

A BUG'S HEAD.

Insects are remarkably well adapted to survive in all kinds of climates, from very hot to very cold. Organs on their heads play a key role in their survival.

PHYSICAL CHARACTERISTICS

Antennae help flying insects detect air currents, vibrations, and even smell. On most insects, antenna can move in all directions. Brushes on some insects' antennae attract mates.

Feelers collect information about the taste and smell of food.

Compound eyes help insects see predators and prey from great distances. Some flying insects also have three smaller "eyes" that are sensitive to light.

Hairs, like the ones sticking out of this millipede, provide weather information and can deter predators.

Some insects have powerful jaws that are used to cut up food, make nests, and dig. Others have sharp tubes that they use for drilling into plants and seeds. Still others have long tongues for sipping nectar.

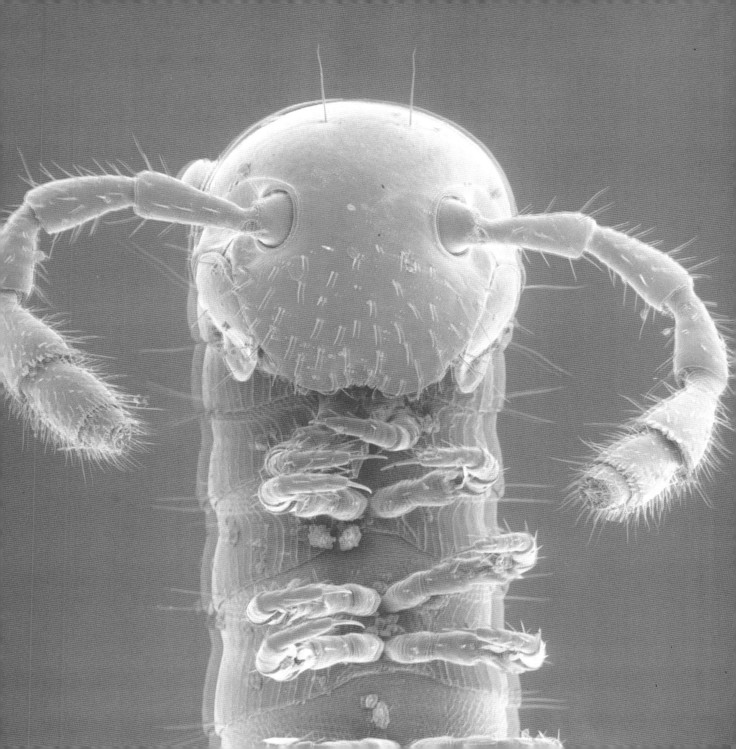

Behind the Scenes

The creepy crawlies in this book were photographed by David Burder, who lives in London, England. He used a special microscope called a Scanning Electron Microscope (S.E.M.). An S.E.M. is about the same size as a baby elephant. David uses an S.E.M. for 3-D photography because the pictures are so much better than if he uses a regular camera.

FUN FACTS ABOUT THIS SPECIAL EQUIPMENT:

Most cameras use light to take pictures. An S.E.M. uses electrons instead.

Electrons don't have color, which is why the S.E.M. pictures are black and white. In this book the black-and-white pictures are printed with red and green inks to increase the 3-D effect.

The S.E.M. operator uses magnets to control the beams of electrons and focus the microscope.

When a creepy crawly is under the microscope, David watches the subject on a television screen. When he sees a screen that he wants to photograph, he pushes a button.

For each picture in this book, David took two photographs of the creepy crawly from different directions.

S.E.M. photography requires teamwork. To make these photographs, David worked with Dr. Peter Evennett, who operated the microscope's controls, and Adrian Hick, who handled the creepy crawlies.